No *Harm* DONE

NURSING HOMES AND RELATED SCENARIOS 1998–2002
A CASE HISTORY

LEAH PALM

To order additional copies of this book, contact:
Xlibris
1-844-714-8691
www.Xlibris.com
Orders@Xlibris.com

ISBN: Softcover   978-1-6641-1949-9
        EBook   978-1-6641-1922-2

Print information available on the last page

Rev. date: 07/31/2020

DEDICATED TO CHRISTINE J. PALM

In memory of her long, enduring, enthusiastic life
January 13, 1910 – August 15, 2002

ACKNOWLEDGMENT

I must thank Linda G. Funderburg, M.D. and Ollie Burnet, teacher, for saying, "You need to share this information with others so they know of what to be aware".

This is the second book for which I am indebted to Fareeda Gibbons for typing and editing the drafts and final copy.

It's also the second book that I am thankful to my publisher Xlibris, 1-888-795-4274, for this completion.

Leah Palm

DEDICATION

To my mother, Christine J. Palm, who suffered the indignities discusses
in this book, and for whom this book was written.

Also it is dedicated to those who read and benefit from the information shared here.

Christine's day at the mall

INTRODUCTION

The following scenarios are presented as though seen through my mother's eyes. She lived in two different nursing homes over a four-year period. She enjoyed learning and sharing with others what she had learned. Her sense of humor and courage carried her through pain and uncertainties. The e first purpose of these scenarios is to share experiences with which I had to work repeatedly for the benefit and protection of my mother. Perhaps they will be helpful to you. The second purpose is to offer options, other than suing, to resolve anger and pain that others cause you and your loved one, through careless, thoughtless words and deeds. The third purpose is to let you know that there are RN's, LVN's aides, maintenance staff, cooks, and other workers, in nursing homes who care greatly about their residents. There just are not enough of them and they get paid very little to do a most difficult physical/emotional job. The fourth purpose is to stimulate your thinking about optional plans in which you can live out your life other than in a nursing home. This is as important as spiritual, pre-need, and financial planning. Finally, the last purpose, is to suggest that no one person can meet all the physical, psychological, social, and leisure requirements of another human being. It takes a family, a family and friends, or perhaps hired caretakers.

Christine, Leah and Friends

Christine and Leah waving "Hello"

NO HARM DONE
Nursing Homes and Related Scenarios
1998-2002

1. I lie in my bed twenty-four hours a day. I cannot sit long enough to leave my room. Nevertheless, my mind is clear and active. I see you walk by my door; you do not look in. You do not wave or give a verbal greeting. You are afraid I will ask you to help me. You offer me no acknowledgment.

    No harm done?

2. Each morning before breakfast, I ask for a moist wash cloth to freshen my face and hands. You ignore me; drop the tray on my table, and say; "I will be right back." You leave and do not return.

    No harm done?

3. I press the call button and wait patiently. I understand that you are busy. A kind housekeeper sees my light, calls me by name, and asks me: "What do you need?" I request she rinse the cleaner off my dentures so I might begin eating. She does so with a smile. I thank her.

    No harm done?

Christine and German Shepherd pup

4.   After breakfast, an aide rushes in. She tells me I must shower today. She grabs my thin arms, lifts and places me in the wheelchair. She rushes me down the hall without my oxygen. I tell her I must have oxygen twenty-four hours a day. She will not listen. She does not understand. She says, "No problem. I will wash you quickly." I begin turning blue in the shower. She panics. I am frightened. Nurses rush in. They hasten me to my room where they attach my oxygen. It takes me three days to recuperate and improve my blood-oxygen level.

No harm done?

5.   I press the call button the following day. You step into the room. I tell you I am experiencing stomach cramping and sharp pains in my lower abdomen. I believe I need an enema. You say, "OK, I will be right back." You leave; your shift ended. You go home. You report discomfort to no one. You do not return the next day; or the next, or the next. You have quit and have taken a job in another nursing home.

No harm done?

6.   Another day, I press my call button. No one answers. I am not incontinent. I know when I need the bedpan. However, the years have weakened my muscles. After approximately forty-five minutes, I must urinate and defecate in my diaper. I am embarrassed and my dignity is separated from me once again. Oh, how I dread the night and week-end shifts.

No harm done?

It's hard to leave friends.

7. At a later time, during a different shift, I press the call button to ask for the removal of my bedpan. It is removed approximately fifty minutes later. It was pressing on my protruding sacrum. My body's bent position was causing excruciating pain to my osteoporotic spinal column. The beginning of a bedsore was being irritated. As a result, I must take additional pain pills that upset my stomach and cause more constipation.

No harm done?

8. Next, I am told that the nursing home will no longer provide individual diapers. They say I must wear "high tech" diapers and share them with other residents. These "high tech" diapers are rough and accordion pleated on the inside where feces can collect. They have a rigid rim that circumscribes each leg and will tear my onion-thin skin. The smallest size is two to three sizes too large for my seventy-eight pounds. My daughter decides I will not wear them. She will provide me individual diapers. An aide/LVN advises my daughter to get them at a discount store. She also suggests the purchase of baby wipes as a helpful means of preventing skin breakdown and possible infection. We thank her.

No harm done?

9. One day, I ask you for my pills that are three hours late. You heave a sigh, and return in half an hour to impatiently thrust a tiny paper cup into my weak, shaking hand; the one with the ring and small finger curled down into the palm. I carefully balance the cup and notice my pink pill is missing. Too late. You have already rushed out.

No harm done?

Christine and Leah on vacation.

10. You are supposed to watch as I take my pills; but you are busy, and I am slow. So, I close one eye as I try to focus with the other, to see the pills in the cup. I steady my free hand around the flimsy plastic cup of water. Then I place the pills in my mouth; drink, and swallow. The sense of touch in my fingers has diminished, and I unknowingly lose another pill in the bedclothes.

No harm done?

11. Since my vision is progressively decreasing, a nurse makes an appointment with my ophthalmologist. An ambulance takes me with my oxygen tank to the physician's office. After being seen, I wait in my wheelchair in front of the appointment desk. It is a small room. There are many patients waiting with me. Suddenly, I realize I have no oxygen. I was not given a full tank. I am only a couple feet from people but I cannot speak loudly enough to draw their attention. My voice has lost its volume because of age and a lack of oxygen. Luckily it is noticed that I am struggling to breathe. I realize I must not go anywhere alone.

No harm done?

12. My physician writes a PRN (as needed) order for Ativan. I am told this is to help curtail my anxiety and fear of suffocation. However, to my LVN, PRN seems to be interpreted as "You do not need to dispense."

No harm done?

Friends

13. Administrative RN's recommend Hospice for me because I am reaching my last days. They know that I will need special support services. Services the nursing home is neither equipped nor staffed to provide. They also know my single daughter has no relatives to help her through my death.

   The request is not approved. Hence, the Hospice twenty-four hour program is delayed. My daughter and I are alone. My daughter learns that Hospice is; "Available as long as your doctor certifies you are terminally ill and you elect to receive these services." Eventually, she obtains the order and learns the significance of selecting a hospice and nurse-friendly physician.

No harm done?

14. The Hospice order delay set up a nightmare of a death event for me and horrendous memories for my daughter. Based on staff comments, the location of my body, and a few gathered facts, my daughter hypothesized the following; I began to suffocate. I panicked as I tried to get attention and get to the doorway. I touched my feet to the floor and my weakened legs gave away. I fell, fractured my pelvis, and lost consciousness. How long I lay on the cold, tile floor, no one knows. It was said, however, that my blood had already coagulated by the time I was found. Again, I must say, I dread the night and weekend shifts.

No harm done?

15. Less than forty-eight hours later, I die. Because of this "accidental death," I have to have an autopsy within forty-eight hours, so my body is rushed to a coroner. Where, neither I nor my daughter knows. The next morning my daughter goes to the funeral home to find me. I am not there. It is then she is told that she must sign a release for the coroner to transfer me to the funeral home.

No harm done?

The Palm Family: Joseph, Christine and Leah Palm

16. Funeral services are held celebrating my 92 years of life; my Boston accent, my courage, and my great sense of humor.

No harm done.

17. However, shortly after my funeral services, my daughter is called by an insensitive, self-serving detective. He asks her to come to his office immediately. The reason he gives, is because he has the next three days off. His call seems important, so my daughter calls a friend who is familiar with legal issues, to accompany her; but no one is home.

No harm done?

18. My daughter is self-sufficient. She drives downtown to the police station expecting to be treated with respect and consideration. In unexpected, horrid detail, during multiple interruptions, in a "matchbox" of an office, the detective advises her of the circumstances and horror of my death.

This includes revealing that the "LVN" who was responsible for me and many others, is not a licensed LVN and should not be dispensing pharmaceuticals and "impersonating a civil servant." In essence, the "LVN" was breaking the law. Th e detective tells my daughter to "initiate a civil suit" and "remember him when she wins her millions."

No harm done?

Promotion day with proud parents

19. In alert-shock, my daughter drives home. Rage, pain, grief, and guilt are surging like tidal waves throughout her body. The detective's words and attitude are processing turbulently in her thoughts. She begins to think ignoble ideas of "suit," and "getting even."

However, she does not know whom to sue; the person who delayed Hospice services, the RN who did not report the behavior of the unlicensed LVN, the young man impersonating an LVN, or the nursing home.

My daughter considers, "Which suit would be a resolution to the ills of the current nursing home problems and which suit would improve the health care within these nursing homes?"

The answer; After consulting a psychiatrist, a police man, and an attorney, the answer was; NONE.

No harm done?

Thanksgiving Day in New York

20. So, is there an alternative action? Possibly. Instead of suing, she meets with the administrators and personnel of the nursing home. The purpose being, to try to resolve the problem of hiring unlicensed health care people. At the meeting she is informed how hiring procedures and personnel have been changed. She is also advised that the unlicensed "LVN" has been fired and his name has been reported to appropriate state authorities.

No harm done.

Friends

21. My daughter and I know, nobody intentionally hired a clever, unlicensed "LVN." No one wished that harm would come to me. However, we do believe that several people in the health care profession and administration were negligent and careless in the handling of their responsibilities.

No harm done?

Home. Junction City Kansas

22. And finally, regarding the "unlicensed LVN," the detective had uncovered different incriminating information from what the state agencies collected. Perhaps the state agencies and the detective needed to communicate with each other regarding the unlicensed LVN. For later, it was quoted to my daughter that the State Nursing Home Agency and the Attorney General, after multiple interviews, interrogations, and review of documentations, came to the illuminating conclusion that there was:

NO HARM DONE!

I AM FREE

"I SOAR WITH THE BIRDS"

"Author Leah Palm"

I SOAR WITH THE BIRDS

I soar with the birds
Orange-breasted, black-winged birds.
Hundreds of birds.
Too numerous to count.

I am free.
Free of bedpans; free of endless waiting.
Free of blindness; free of deafness.
Free of trembling hands.

Wait. I see people.
Non-existing people.
They come and go.
They are silent.

Nevertheless, I am not afraid.
It is spring.
And I soar with the birds.
Orange-breasted, black-winged birds.

Christine J. Palm

May, 2002

The End.

Printed in the United States
By Bookmasters